The Hour of Love

Piyush Singh

BookLeaf
Publishing

India | USA | UK

Presentation by *BookLeaf Publishing*

Web: www.bookleafpub.com

E-mail: info@bookleafpub.com

ISBN:9789358310993

First edition 2024

DEDICATION

This book is dedicated to those who have dared
to love fiercely, to navigate the treacherous
waters of distance, and to embrace the fragile
beauty of the human heart. It is for the
dreamers, the seekers, and the believers in the
transformative power of love's hour.

To the souls who have experienced the depths
of longing and the heights of passion, this
collection is for you. Your resilience,
vulnerability, and unwavering hope have
inspired the verses that grace these pages.

To those who have weathered the storms of
grief and loss, know that you are not alone.
May these poems offer solace, healing, and a
reminder that love's hour can coexist with
sorrow, leading us to emerge stronger and more
compassionate.

To the romantics who revel in stolen moments
and shared intimacy, this collection celebrates
the magic that resides in the spaces between

two beating hearts. May these words ignite sparks of connection, and may you find echoes of your own experiences within these pages.

To the dreamers who dare to believe in the power of love, may this collection be a testament to the resilience of the human spirit. May it remind you that within the complexities of love, hope and joy can flourish, lighting our way through the darkest of nights.

Lastly, I dedicate this book to the eternal essence of love itself. To its ability to transcend time, distance, and circumstance, weaving threads of connection that bind us all. May love's hour forever inspire us to cherish and nurture the relationships that shape our lives.

With gratitude and reverence, I offer this collection to you, dear reader. May these words serve as a companion, a mirror, and a source of inspiration on your own journey through the intricate labyrinth of the human heart.

Piyush Kumar Singh

PREFACE

In the timeless realm of poetry, where words have the power to transcend boundaries and touch the deepest recesses of our souls, "The Hour of Love" emerges as an intimate invitation into the labyrinth of emotions that lie at the core of the human experience. Within these pages, you will embark on a journey of self-discovery, exploring the delicate interplay of love, distance, hope, grief, romance, and intimacy.

Poetry has long been a vessel through which we navigate the vast ocean of human emotions, seeking solace, understanding, and connection. In "The Hour of Love," the author fearlessly delves into the depths of their own heart and invites you to join them on this intimate exploration. Through evocative imagery and lyrical craftsmanship, they invite you to bear witness to the intricate tapestry of their emotions, baring their soul in vulnerable and resonant verse.

In the opening lines, you will be transported to the realm of distance, where the ache of separation reverberates through the verses. The author masterfully captures the essence of longing, weaving delicate threads of hope that bridge the divide between hearts. As you delve deeper, you will encounter the multifaceted facets of love itself – its euphoria, its vulnerability, and the enduring connections it forges.

Grief, an inevitable companion on the journey of life, finds its poignant place in these pages. With profound sensitivity and heartfelt expression, the author guides you through the labyrinth of loss, offering solace and understanding to those who have traversed the winding path of heartbreak. Amidst the shadows, they illuminate the way towards healing and resilience, reminding us that love's hour can coexist with sorrow.

Romance and intimacy blossom in vibrant hues within these verses. You will be swept away by the intoxicating dance of two souls, entwined in the electric currents of passion. Each word, carefully chosen, creates a symphony of emotions that resonates within your own heart, invoking memories of stolen glances, whispered promises, and the transformative power of shared connection.

"The Hour of Love" is a deeply personal and universal testimony to the beauty and complexity of the human heart. It is an exploration of our shared experiences, our collective vulnerabilities, and our innate desire to connect with one another. In these poems, you will find fragments of your own journey, fragments that resonate, console, and inspire.

May this collection serve as a companion on your own quest for understanding and self-discovery. May these words provide solace during moments of longing, ignite sparks of hope amidst darkness, and remind you that within the depths of love's hour, you are never alone. Embrace the emotions that dance across these pages, for within them lies the essence of what it means to be human.

With an open heart, immerse yourself in the enchanting world of "The Hour of Love" and let its melodies echo within you, leaving an indelible imprint that will accompany you long after the final page is turned.

Piyush Kumar Singh

Table of Contents

Eternal Love

For you my love, I will die a thousand times
and be born a thousand more
until I'm made in your image.

A Galaxy Full of Love

Encapsulated, engulfed by the presence
which extends miles beyond your body.
I am wrapped in a feeling that consumes all
of me yet makes me different from what
I used to be. Together we are infinite
and in your arms I am born like
a galaxy full of million stars.

Bare in Love

3

Stripped down to our bones,
we hang all our faces on the door.
Inside, you and I, we exist faceless,
bare and true to the selves we love
and accepted one another without judgment.

Love's Memorial

A river parts into tears and agony.
Our pieces crumble, falling into a void of
uncertainty.
Why shall this day pass? And why must we walk
past our memorial that still keeps the flowers
alive?

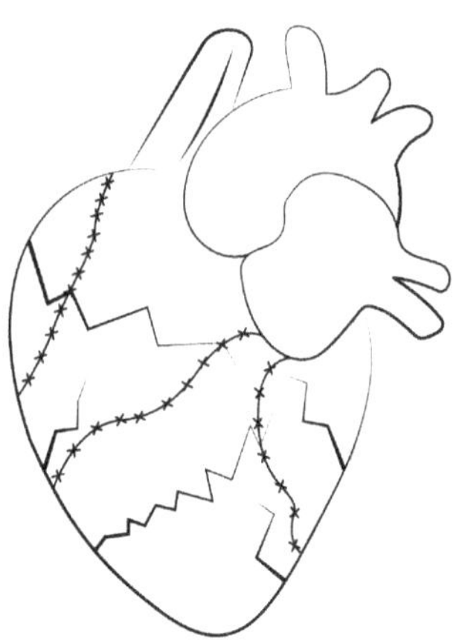

Fused in Love

5

Sculpted by the fading lips, this face you have, is no different from my own.

I've known this since the time you whispered, "I am you, you are me."

The world sees us differently, yet we see each other in love, indistinguishable, wearing the same face, same soul.

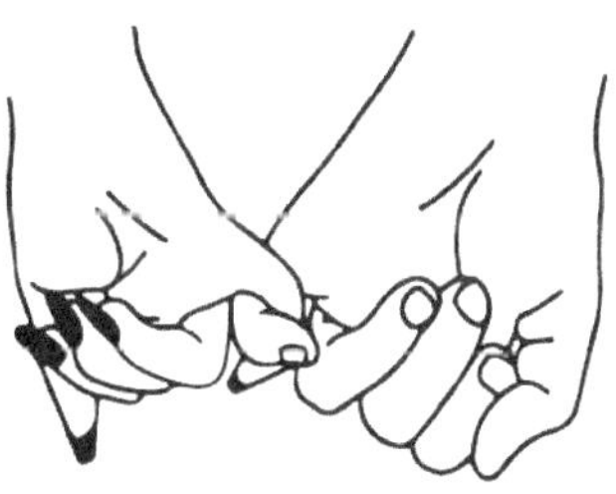

Marked by Love

Why depart?
Like the sun,
like winters,
like dew on the green,
like words when I am listening,
Why not arrive? Like love that marks me home.

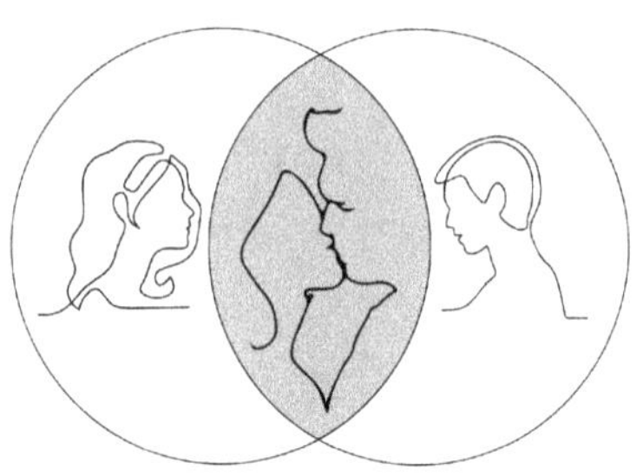

Lovesick

Why do smiles end in grief?
Yesterday was a day that passed but that's not
today.
Today I feel empty in a room full of memories.
I am awake from my dream, you are missing,
loneliness bears your name and I am her lover.
You loved me so, that I do not know what to feel
when you aren't here.

The Crimson Love

8

The crimson of my wall reflects on me, all red.
We rolled in the sewers of hope,
we drowned in the sludge, all black.
And in the nothingness of time
we lost our eyes which dreamt of a different life.

The Unyielding Love

Stirred by your eyes,
overflown by your presence.
Take these words which echo
inside like a devotion,
make me arch and then
break the convictions which
bend my mind to an unreal hope.
you and I, our bodies pass weightless
in the bloom of an unyielding love.

The Ephemeral Love

Shreds of moments passed, mostly warm, falls in
winter.
Melts on our skin, now cold, now forsaken for
lack of a roof.
Without a home, we are just travelers who
passed each other.
For sometime we saw and now an eternity to
spend in blindness.

Shades of Love

Without you,
I would never know
the rainbow between
a smile and a moan.

A Hopeless Love

Drained of hope,
eyes lament the
lack of your shape.
Doors left open,
robbed every night
A distorted tomorrow
remains, a husk of what
a 'Home' is supposed to be.

The Circle of Love

This part of me
exists in you.
Invisible to me,
better than my own.
A part of me that
has been inside you.
To see you walk towards
me all your life.
To seek this part of you
I've held through many lives
This union isn't for bodies,
but for the little parts that
we carried for each of us
to find and embrace.
To feel whole again.

Love-less Tomorrow

Don't let me pass from your arms,
from your voice that holds my heart.
The pain burns and the arson
is set by a loveless tomorrow.
Drift not into a day where I don't see you,
where life finds no clock to count the hours
before sunrise.

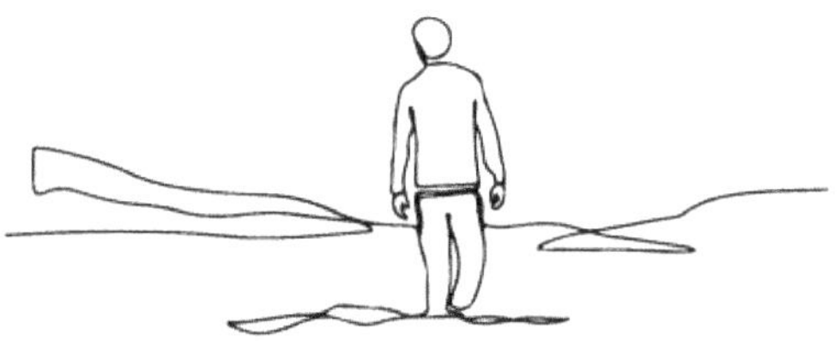

Love's Hold

15

What hold do you have?
Safe or trapped? Doesn't matter.
Held in a space which feels home,
held in a way which feels warm.
Your hold is as good as the life
that holds my body to my soul.
Held through the fabric of time and lives,
held together just right

Depths of Love

Deep within you
bury me, silently
with tears, with smile
with blood and with words
For me to bloom, let yourself
be my earth.

Infinite Love

17

Be limitless in love,
because everything else
might just have an end.

Etched in Love

18

If you let me,
I'll leave a page blank.
because when my lips
are done etching, you will
have a story that's worth
a million lifetimes.

Drunk in love

Pour me a little something
they call 'love' and let me
have it straight and neat.
Let it burn my insides, let it
purge my emptiness and
fill it with nothingness.
Pour me a shot of life,
I want to taste something
even more bitter than death.

Blown Away in Love

Villainy in our charms
oscillates between charades.
Heroes fight a losing war,
we started dead, maybe
someday we will be alive.
Until then kamikaze hearts
rot in the pale of the night
and blows in hope, leaving
bits of the city they built
Everyday.

A Hope called Love

21

Even when you aren't here,
you remain in my words.
This inevitable love
is also immutable.
Invincible, untouched
by the cruel hands of time.

Prisoners of Love

Tamed by your Love,
a wildfire contained
in your gentle touch.
I burn in your hearth,
I rise in your eyes.
Impenetrable love
holds us captive in a
room full of desires
smoldering till dawn.

Mirrored in Love

Your fingers reach
where no lips, no being
other than you reached.
To be with you is to be
with my own self.
To love you is to love
my own self.

Cosmic Love

With you time is a slow burn.
No gaps between our souls,
no earth between our sky.
A thousand stars die and a
thousand are born in the cosmic
celebration that happens in
the folds of your arms.

Love's Karma

Putty to my fingers,
mirror to my soul.
I raise grand castles
and you tell me how
to annihilate them
wall by wall.
Night is not above us,
night is in our bones
that grinds together to
make us moan in cycles of
construction and destruction.

Stripped in Love

Proximity of bodies doesn't
bring two people closer.
And I can tell when
I'm close to you there is an
alignment of thoughts,
of emotions, of flow.
A sense of home,
a sense of safety,
a sense of being here with you,
seeing you naked in all your truths
That is when we are closest to one another.

The Spell of Love

Drawn to no end,
I'm not sane in your presence.
In your presence I'm love that
brims out of your lips.
I surrender to the force that
your eyes exert, opening every
inch of my skin to be a receptor
to your love.

The 'ifs' and 'buts' of love

We are not who we were.
Set in an endless drift we
float away from each other.
How long can we resist the
constant push of the world?
Love anchors us more in
imagination than in reality.
Time passes and maybe
our love will too, maybe it
was always a tombstone
meant to hold 'what could
have been' if we had known
each other in a different time,
in a different life.

Written in Love

If you let me,
I'll leave a page blank,
because when my lips are done etching,
you'll have a story worth a million lifetimes.

Given in Love

Scrape my heart as long as you can,
we don't have an eternity, take what
you must and as much as you can.
The void you'll leave will tell how you
loved me deep enough to scrape
from a heart of stone.

The Masterstroke of Love

What of the love that made me?
With every stroke of your gilded lips
my being came to be.
And this novel me who breathes
what was given from your lungs.
A skin that lustres,
branded with your sliding fingers.
This infusion dilutes my
soul completely with your essence.
I don't know who I am anymore,
Am I you, or are you me?

The Embers of Love

Enlightened bodies molded in love.
You and I drown in amber delights.
Cast away by the light we dance in the dark.
Floating over your name, my name shines in
each of your sighs.

The Deceit of Love

I've been a host to this ugliness
that others call beauty.
I've learnt to make others feel
what I no more feel.
To make them see how striking
my scar is, to let them follow the
pieces of my broken heart.

The Sands of Love

Things slipping from hold.
What's trust if not sand?
We reached the grip that
locked us in a cathartic decay.
The uneven pull, and my
elastic skin now melts in disdain.
I stretch, reshape never to be what
I was before the carmine flames.

Love's Conduit

Flow in me like a gentle curl.
There are parts of me that ache to be
swayed by your wanting words.
This skin isn't all of me, neither my eyes,
nor my lips. But through them,
you can reach the deepest trench
of the ocean that I am.

Salvation in Love

What of it, this thought that doesn't feel vile.
I've imagined our bodies intertwined in sacred
sins.
But tell me, why does it seem like liberation?
Can our bodies speak for the silence of locked
lips?
Why do I feel that the honey which drips from
your wanting lips is enough to fill my empty
soul?

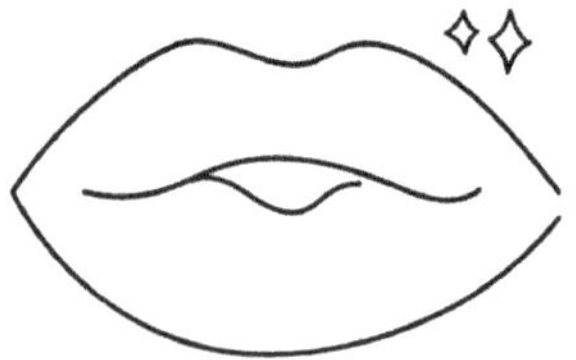

Open Wide in Love

37

Spread my shame to
find my naked desire.
Place your words in the
beads of my rushed breath.
Stay inside my ghost,
till I am one with your famished soul.

Unravelled in Love

This love, a river that floods our mind.
Ego washed, shame lost,
perverse thoughts, lewd acts unlocked,
a beast unleashed, a city set on fire.
Love unites in light and dark alike,
to be naked without a care,
to be indecent like fools.
To love is to be wild, to unravel
and to be unsophisticated.

Torrential Love

Gushed, when it rained plenty,
the barriers broke, the hearts raced.
Pages spread, bodies overwritten,
rules broken; revolution ushered.
In our quest to find hallowed ground
we found unclaimed land,
we stayed, we called it home.
Storms came, we stayed.

Love-Less

Almost love, something less.
Marred by the night that lurks in the day.
Do I hide in the shadows?
Am I invisible to your watery eyes?
Do we stand on green grass
or are we slipping endlessly on
an impossible slope?

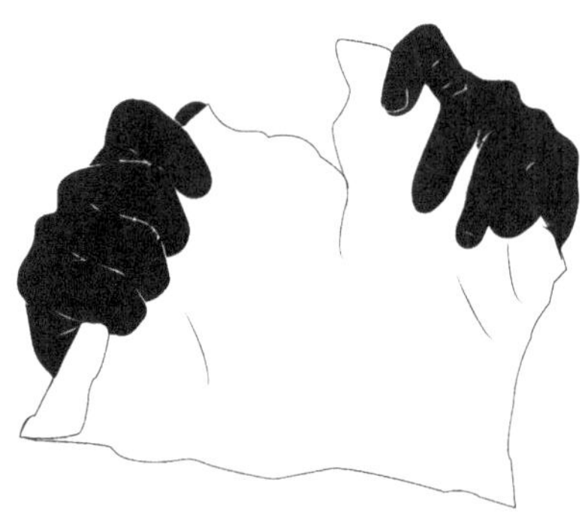

The Feast of Love

The way you feast leaves me initiated,
for more night,
for more storms
for more dare.
It's true, you turn me
into an endless chasm
to be filled by your insatiable soul.

Moth to my Love

The last of the turning moths,
fall prey to a perilous tongue.
To the sun, she says.
Burn your heart and grow another one.
Blend with a smile and flutter like a butterfly.
Deep dive into my dark void.
If you make it back,
tell me, how do they fare?
The pretty things I've dumped there,
each with a slice of my heart.
Bring me toys, I've broken in delight,
some I got tired of,
some I foraged for the insides.
Tell me what say those, who lie
waiting for a rope from my eyes.
And I know who murdered who,
for I've often tasted blood in my food.
But this I can tell you,
Only a few have survived my longest night.

Twisted Love

Tell me, have you not
felt the bitterness off my lips?
A lingering aftertaste of agony?

Tell me, have you not
felt the unyielding grip
of my fondling hands?
A red mark of undying fury?

There are days, I want to
pass this piercing torment
onto your capitulating soul.

There are ways I sow tears
into your blooming moons.

Some days, I build my palace
over your bleeding parts.

Even though it is you
inside my crumbling heart.

Impossible Love

Arrived after our time.
Drowning now, when
I am too shallow.
Yearning, breaking
for the non-existent.
Lover divine,
you are a constant
who can never be mine.

The Epitaph of Love

45

A river parts into tears and agony.
Our pieces crumble
falling into a void of uncertainty.
Why shall this day pass?
And why we must walk
past our memorial that
still keeps the flower alive?

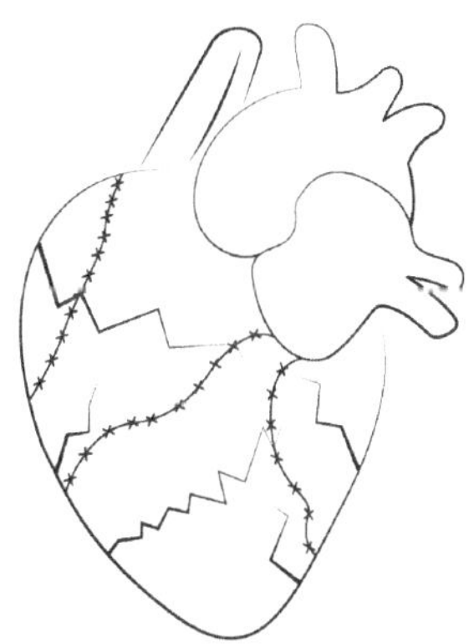

Love-ache

Today, undo me.
Taste what drips in the name of sin.
Pull down the threads off my wanton skin.
Lay your fingers where it burns the most.
Place your lips where the sun never kisses.
Savor the revelations of an unholy night.
And when our bodies tremble in this
beautiful ache, listen to our souls say,
"Encore!"

The Promised Love

Promise me time,
Not just this fleeting moment.
We might fail to be but to
stand together today and here
intertwines us in a sacred destiny
Promise me land which starts
from you and ends in sunsets
from many different windows
and not just the one where we met.
What's good in being mine if
we can't share the same space
where we breathe life together.

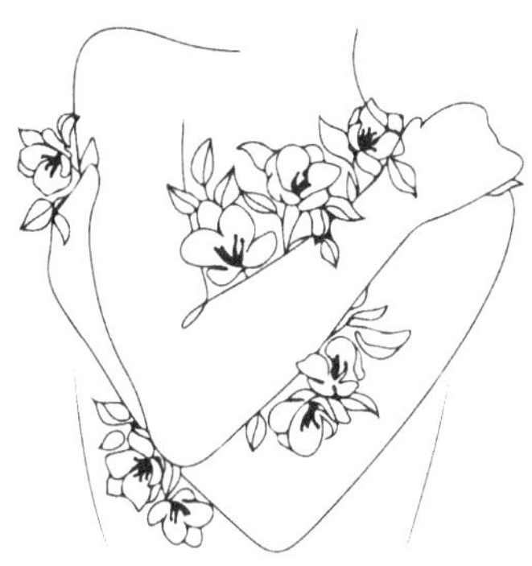

YOU, whom I love

48

Days have passed,
your eyes still speak mystery.
The otherness that you are
frightens me and allures me,
all the same.

A Little of Love

49

When you go,
Let me keep,
a little of memories,
a little of happiness,
a little of tears,
a little of you.
because when you go,
you'll take a little of me
forever.

Lovenomics

50

Hard bites, soft lips.
Painted with sweet deceit.
To taste your lies, I've kissed you hard.
To taste your soul, I've loved you slow.
To make you mine, I've lost my own.